Healing

The Children's Bread

Dr. Murl Edward Gwynn

Healing – The Children's Bread
Copyright © 2013 by Dr. Murl Edward Gwynn

Published by MEG Enterprises Publications
PO Box 2165
Reidsville, GA 30453
(912) 557-6507
meg@kencable.net
www.murlgwynn.com

Unless otherwise identified, Scripture quotations are from the Holy Bible New International Version, copyright © 1973, 1978, 1984 by International Bible Society. Zondervan Publishing House. Used by permission.

Scripture quotations marked KJV are from the King James Version of the Bible.

Scripture taken from the New King James Version®. Copyright © 1982 by Thomas Nelson, Inc. Used by permission. All rights reserved.

All rights reserved. No part of this book may be reproduced or transmitted in any form or by any means without written permission from the author.

ISBN 978-0-9711766-3-8

Also by Dr. Gwynn

Easter-Not What You Think

Chrislam – What Communion Hath Light With Darkness?

Conflict – Christianity's Love vs. Islam's Submission

The President Was a Good Man

Anything for Acceptance

The gods Among Us

Table of Contents

Preface vii
Chapter 1 Entrance of Death 1
Chapter 2 Healing is God's Plan 7
Chapter 3 Healing and Atonement 15
Chapter 4 As it is in Heaven 21
Chapter 5 The Ingredients of God's Will 31
Chapter 6 Man Doesn't Live By Bread Alone 53
Chapter 7 The Children's Bread 59
Chapter 8 The Commission 69
Chapter 9 Conclusion 75

Preface

This book comes from my own observations, experiences, and scripture consumption.

By no means am I an authority on healing, whether natural or spiritual. I am a sojourner with fellow saints seeking the perfect that God gave us through His Son, Jesus.

I have come to realize that God by no means ever intended for mankind to suffer physical and emotional sickness of any kind. His will was demonstrated in the creation process from the very beginning. Everything was good, everything was harmonious, and everything flowed with the commonality of perfection with no sickness, pain, or sin.

Sin entered the earth and into all men by means of Adam's rebellion. That rebellion removed man from the perfect and brought dysfunction of all kinds. It brought decay, disease, doubt, and delusion, of which no one would be free without intercession and an intercessor.

As a Christian, believing in a loving and forgiving God, seeing much pain, heartache and sickness, it didn't make sense to me that a loving God would want His children suffering the tragedies of sin's wages. After all, God made a way from mankind's sins through the suffering and death of His Son. Wouldn't that same God also make a way for the physical and emotional suffering of those same humans that His Son died for? It just makes sense that He did! I believe I have realized the answer. It is found in Jesus!

Knowing that healing is found in Jesus is not enough to receive and walk in healing. We must believe that healing is for us, God's wants our bodies, mind, and soul healed, and that kingdom perfection is meant for us.

Only as we firmly and faithfully stand on God's promises will we realize that healing is the children's bread.

1

Entrance of Death

I have found that most Christians do not fully understand the implications of man's fall in the Garden of Eden when Adam and Eve rebelled against God's perfect plan for their lives.

We understood that when Adam ate of the forbidden tree he brought sin into the world and everything became corrupt bringing death and disease. We came to understand that Jesus was the promised child, the "he" in Genesis 3:15. [1] However we mostly saw the promised child as a spiritual savior but missed the other redeeming

---

[1] Gen 3:14 So the Lord God said to the serpent, "Because you have done this, "Cursed are you above all the livestock and all the wild animals! You will crawl on your belly and you will eat dust all the days of your life. 15 And I will put enmity between you and the woman, and between your offspring and hers; he will crush your head, and you will strike his heel." NIV

realities that Jesus came to restore. Our focus was on being forgiven for our sins and being brought back to a right relationship with Father God for eternity. What we failed to realize is that what Jesus did for us on the cross and then resurrection was for the entire person and not just his soul. Jesus came to restore everything that was lost through Adam's sin.

Every Christian would accept the fact that the moment Adam sinned death entered the world. Man lost fellowship with God and man became subject to the perversion of earth's corruption by Satan. Death entered, sickness became a fact of life, and everyone, no one left out, would fall prey to a slow death.

We know that God told Adam that if he rebelled, or ate of the forbidden tree he would die. Actually God said *"In dying you will die!"* Sickness is a part of that *dying you will die* reality, because sin brings death and from death sickness in all forms eats away at our bodies and minds.

Perfection

We must fully understand what the earth was like before Adam's rebellion. Remember, God said that everything He had created was *good*.² There was no corruption of any kind, everything was perfect, strong, healthy, and full of vigor. Everything worked in harmony with God's will and perfect plan to accomplish as God intended to bring about joy, happiness, and prosperity in all forms. Death could not operate before Adam's rebellion because everything was controlled by the perfection of God's will, it all flowed in conformity as God intended.

Before the rebellion every cell in every living thing responded to how it was made. It all was made to function by divine plan, purpose, and to reproduce of its kind. As long as perfection was the rule everything would function as God had made it. Everything was made to interact with other created things whether flesh and blood, or earth and stone.

Adam, being the ruler of the earth³ and operating in a perfect state without sin, knew no

---

² Gen 1:31 God saw all that he had made, and it was very good. And there was evening, and there was morning — the sixth day. NIV

³ Gen 1:26 Then God said, "Let us make man in our image, in our likeness, and let them rule over the fish of the sea and the birds of the air, over the livestock, over all the earth, and over all the creatures that move along the ground." 27 So God created man in his own image, in

sickness, disease, or imperfections. He was made *good*, but had the capacity to make choice. His choice could insure that God's plan would be fulfilled or it could be thwarted. Sadly, Adam chose wrongly.

However, before Adam's rebellion everything in the universe reflected God's will, just as it is in God's kingdom in the unseen world. Heaven is God's domain, His kingdom functions in a harmonious and perfect state of being. It is always in a now state of perfection and cannot be tainted by sin, disease, or other impurities. That is what God wanted for mankind through Adam. God's will in His kingdom is perfection, holiness, and righteousness and that is what He intended for Adam and his offspring.

When Adam rebelled, and because he was the ruler of earth and willfully listened to Satan, who encouraged him to rebel, he lost his authority to

---

the image of God he created him; male and female he created them. 28 God blessed them and said to them, "Be fruitful and increase in number; fill the earth and subdue it. Rule over the fish of the sea and the birds of the air and over every living creature that moves on the ground." NIV rule.[4] Under the new ruler (Satan) of the earth everything became like its new master. It became corrupt, sickly, and death ridden.[5] Under Adam, before the rebellion, when he was perfect and *good,* everything functioned as God intended. There was nothing that was different than what God willed as it was in heaven.

We can see then, that God willed for earth, under Adam and his offspring, to be just like it was in heaven. God intended the earth and humans to realize heaven on earth in all forms and function. When Adam sinned he lost authority, ruling rights, and opened the door for earth's new master to promote his personality and lifestyle. It became sick in all forms, it soon began to decay, and corruption ruled.

We can see then that perfection was lost. Sin brought death, death brought sickness, and the

---

[4] Rom 6:16 Don't you know that when you offer yourselves to someone to obey him as slaves, you are slaves to the one whom you obey — whether you are slaves to sin, which leads to death, or to obedience, which leads to righteousness? NIV

[5] Rom 5:12 Therefore, just as sin entered the world through one man, and death through sin, and in this way death came to all men, because all sinned— NIV

ongoing reality for man was that he lost the perfect state that God intended.

A Perfect Plan

God was not without a plan. God knew what would be done to ensure that His perfect plan for mankind would be realized. As mentioned earlier, God ensured that another Adam would be born in the earth to redeem mankind and bring back God's will for the earth as it is in heaven.[6]

---

[6] 1 Cor 15:45 And so it is written, "The first man Adam became a living being." The last Adam became a life-giving spirit. NKJV

1 Cor 15:21-23 For since by man came death, by Man also came the resurrection of the dead. 22 For as in Adam all die, even so in Christ all shall be made alive. NKJV

2

Healing is God's Plan

THE BIBLICAL BASIS OF HEALING IN THE OLD TESTAMENT

The Genesis record contains two accounts of divine healing. In Genesis 17:18-19, God promised to heal Sara's barrenness. In Genesis 21:1-7 this was fulfilled. Genesis 20:17 records the healing of Abimelech.

In the book of Exodus, disease and divine healing more clearly enter the Biblical record. After the deliverance of Israel from Egypt, the people marched for several days without finding water. When they finally came to Marah, they could not drink the water because it was bitter. God showed Moses a tree which, when cast into the waters, made the waters sweet.

Following this God revealed Himself as Healer of His people. He said: "...If thou wilt diligently hearken to the voice of the Lord thy God, and wilt do that which is right in His sight, and wilt give ear to His commandments, and keep all His statues, I will put none of these diseases upon thee, which I have brought upon the Egyptians; for I am the Lord that healeth thee." (Exodus 15:26) A more accurate translation of this is "I am the Lord your physician." This indicates a habitual, continuing action.

Because this promise was first given to Israel in a specific situation, some say it applies only to them and that Christians cannot claim it. We must remember, however, that the names of God are revelations of His nature and character, and God does not change. If He was by nature a physician and healer then, He is the same today.

Other specific references to healing in Exodus are the healing of Moses' leprous hand

(Exodus 4:1-7) and God's promise to take away sickness from among his people (Exodus 23:25).

The book of Leviticus might be called the "health care manual" of the Bible. God reveals regulations regarding the treatment of disease (for an example see Leviticus 13:1-46; 14:1-32) and gives directives regarding healthy living (see Leviticus 15:1-33 for an example).

The book of Numbers records the healing of the leprosy of Miriam and Aaron (Numbers 12:1-15) and the healing of plagues that affected Israel (Numbers 16:41-50 and 21:5-9).

Deuteronomy 28 is a very important chapter related to healing. It explains the relation of obedience to physical health. Other passages in Deuteronomy stressing this truth include 7:15; 29:22; 30:20.

Manoah's wife was healed of barrenness in Judges 13:2-24.

There are several records of healings in the book of 1 Kings. There are stories about a man with the withered hand in 1 Kings 13:4-6 and the raising of a dead child in 1 Kings 17:17-24. The record continues in 2 Kings with the healing of a child by Elisha in 2 Kings 4:8-37 and the healing of Naaman in 2 Kings 5:1-14. Study also the case of King Azariah in 2 Kings 15:1-12. From the healing of Hezekiah in 2 Kings 20:1-11 we learn that God can heal terminal illness and add years to life (see also 2 Chronicles 32:24-26 and Isaiah 38:1-12,16). We also learn from 2 Kings 13:14 and 21 that death comes to all men, even those with a ministry of healing.

A great prayer of repentance related to healing is recorded in 2 Chronicles 6:26-31. II Chronicles 20:9 promises that God hears when we cry in affliction. In 2 Chronicles 16, you can read the story of Asa who died because he did not seek healing from God. His sin was not going to medical doctors, but ignoring God and His healing power. In 2 Chronicles 26, you can read about

Uzziah's leprosy, and in 2 Chronicles 30:20, of the healing of the people through the prayers of Hezekiah.

The book of Job, especially Chapters 1 and 2 permits us to see behind the scenes to identify the source of Job's problems, including his sickness.

The book of Psalms contains many promises, revelations, and prayers concerning healing.

Study the following passages: The book of Proverbs provides wisdom regarding healthy living. Proverbs 3:7-8 explains how to be healthy. Proverbs 4:20-23 reveals that the issues of life are affected by the heart attitude and that God's promises bring life and health. Proverbs 15:4 and 30 confirm that wholesome talk results in health and Proverbs 16:24 show that God's Word brings healing. Proverbs 16:24 indicates that the Word of God brings healing to the bones, and Proverbs 17:22 reveals the physical effects of spiritual problems.

Ecclesiastes 3:3 confirms that there is a set time for healing, and Ecclesiastes 5:17 demonstrates how sorrow and wrath are related to sickness.

Isaiah 6:10 explains the relationship between spiritual understanding, conversion, and healing. Isaiah 19:22 confirms that when God is entreated He heals ("entreat" means to "ask earnestly and solicit pressingly"). Isaiah 32:3-4 is a great prophetic promise of healing being part of the Kingdom of God. Isaiah 33:24 and 35:5-6 tells of healing during the Millennium and how the inhabitants will say "I am not sick."

In Isaiah 53:5, we are promised healing and deliverance through the atonement. Isaiah 57:18-19 encourages us to draw near for healing, and Isaiah 58:8 confirms that our "health shall spring forth." In Isaiah 61:1, we learn that Jesus was sent to bind up the brokenhearted. This speaks of an inner, emotional healing.

In Jeremiah 8:14-15; 20-22, the bitterness of sin is tied to physical illness, and Jeremiah 15:18 explains how to deal with an incurable wound. Jeremiah 17:14; 30:12-17; and 33:6 confirms God is the source of healing.

Lamentations 3:33 confirms that "God does not willingly afflict."

Ezekiel 17:14; 30:17; and 33:6 confirm that God can heal and restore health. Ezekiel 30:12-13 speaks of incurable wounds medicine cannot heal. Only spiritual healing can cure these types of wounds. Ezekiel 34: 4, 16, 21 and Zechariah 11:16 contain warnings to shepherds (spiritual leaders) who have ignored the sick sheep (people).

Daniel Chapter 4 records King Nebuchadnezzar's sickness and healing. Hosea 5:13 warns of the danger of going elsewhere for healing, and Hosea 6:1 and 7:1 confirm that God can and will heal both physical and spiritual conditions.

Hosea 11:3 records God's sad words about Israel: "They knew not that I healed them." The Old Testament record of healing closes with the promise in Malachi 4:2 that Jesus will arise with "healing in His wings."

OLD TESTAMENT NAMES OF GOD:

Jehovah-Jireh - The Lord will provide Genesis 22:14 NT: Philippians 4:19

Jehovah-Nissi - The Lord our banner Exodus 17:8-15 NT: John 15:13

Jehovah-Shalom - The Lord our peace Judges 6:24 NT: Ephesians 2:14

Jehovah-Raah - The Lord our shepherd Psalms 23:1 NT: John 10:11

Jehovah-Tsidkenu - The Lord our righteousness Jeremiah 23:6 NT: I Corinthians 1:30

Jehovah-Shammah - The Lord is present Ezekiel 48:35 NT: Hebrews 13:5

Jehovah-Rapha - The Lord thy Physician Exodus 15:26 NT: James 5:15

3

Healing and Atonement

"Surely, He hath borne our griefs, and carried our sorrows; yet we did esteem Him stricken, smitten of God, and afflicted. But He was wounded for our transgressions, He was bruised for our iniquities; the chastisement of our peace was upon Him; and with His stripes we are healed." (Isaiah 53:45)

Isaiah 53 is a prophetic chapter referring to Jesus Christ. Verses four and five definitely link healing to the atonement of Jesus by His death on the cross. The only use of the word "surely" in this chapter, which is a word of emphasis, precedes this provision for our salvation and healing.

Sin and sickness are Satan's twin evils. Salvation and healing are God's twin provisions for deliverance. Before Calvary people were saved and healed by looking forward to it in faith. Afterwards, salvation and healing comes by looking back to it in faith.

Disease and death entered by sin and are penalties for iniquity, so their remedy must be found in the atonement of Christ. Jesus bore your sicknesses and carried your diseases at the same time and in the same manner that He bore your sins. *"That it might be fulfilled which was spoken by Esaias the prophet, saying, Himself took our infirmities and bare our sicknesses."* (Matthew 8:17)

God laid both sin and sickness on Jesus in the same atonement. Peter speaks of salvation and healing as being an accomplished fact: *"Who His own self bare our sins in His own body on the tree, that we, being dead to sins, should live unto righteousness: by whose stripes ye were healed."* (1 Peter 2:24)

Since Jesus bore your sins, it must be God's will to save when you come to Him. Since He bore your sicknesses, it must also be His will to heal when you come to Him. The same God who forgives all your sin also heals all your diseases: *"Bless the Lord, O my soul, and forget not all His benefits: Who forgiveth all thine iniquities, who healeth all thy diseases."* (Psalms 103:2-3)

The redemptive name "Jehovah-tsidkenu" reveals God's redemptive provision for your soul.

The redemptive name "Jehovah-rapha" reveals His redemptive provision for your body.

The word "saved" in Romans 10:9 is the same word used by Mark when he said, "as many as touched him were made whole."

The Greek word "sozo" used in these passages means salvation from sin and its penalty. Sickness is part of the penalty, so salvation is part of the atonement for sin.

While the atonement of Christ has guaranteed the believer's final perfection, both physical and spiritual human imperfections continue. The believer continues to suffer attacks of sin and sickness. The ultimate benefits of Christ's atonement are yet to be revealed. We are..."...*kept by the power of God through faith unto salvation ready to be revealed in the last time.*" (1 Peter 1:5)

The benefits of salvation to be revealed in eternity are those of physical and spiritual perfection. We still battle sin and sickness while we are in this world.

There is a past, present, and future tense of salvation:

- Past: You are saved from the penalty of sins committed in the past.

- Present: You are saved from the power of sin in the present.

- Future: You will be saved from the presence of sin in the future (eternity).

The same is true of healing. You are saved from the penalty of sickness for your sin. You can overcome the power of disease in the present time and be saved from the actual presence of disease in eternity. Since healing is a benefit of the atonement, you should accept Jesus not only as Savior, but also as Healer.

How can He keep you from sin if you have never accepted Him as Savior? How can He keep you from sickness if you have never accepted Him as Healer?

4

As it is in Heaven

In this manner, therefore, pray: Our Father in heaven, Hallowed be Your name. 10 Your kingdom come. Your will be done On earth as it is in heaven. 11 Give us this day our daily bread. 12 And forgive us our debts, As we forgive our debtors. 13 And do not lead us into temptation, But deliver us from the evil one. For Yours is the kingdom and the power and the glory forever. Amen. Matthew 6:9

When Jesus taught His disciples to pray, using words like the ones in the Lord's Prayer, He was not commanding them to repeat something without substance.

First of all, He was not telling them to repeat anything. He was telling to them to pray with a heavenly understanding.

Second, Jesus constantly taught the disciples about the Kingdom of Heaven, the Kingdom of God, and Kingdom principles.

The Kingdom of Heaven:

The Kingdom of heaven is the abode of God. It is a physical place where born-again humans will go once they die. It has substance, it operates through the system of God's will (Kingdom of God), and it functions in perfection.

In the Kingdom of heaven there is no lack, poverty, turmoil, corruption, darkness, infirmity, disease, death, or sickness.

The inhabitants of the Kingdom of heaven are made up of good angels, born-again people, Jesus, Holy Spirit, and Father God.

The Kingdom of heaven is the true picture, example, and manifestation of how God wants all of creation to operate and manifest *good*. It is the manifestation of the good that was in the Garden of Eden before man sinned.

The Kingdom of God:

The Kingdom of God is the manifestation of God's will in government form in all aspects. Government in the sense that it has order, a head, and controlling group of characters that carry out God's will.

Jesus taught that the Kingdom of God was to touch every aspect of human existence. He taught that God's *will* must be the directing factor in mankind's desires, joys, and longings.

The Kingdom of God is most evident in man when he faithfully seeks to be governed by God and is under the tutelage of the Holy Spirit.

Kingdom Principles

Kingdom principles are the supernatural principles that God uses to bring about His will.

Jesus taught that when mankind obeys God's word they will fulfill righteousness and walk in the *good* that God intended from the beginning of creation.

It is a kingdom principle that faith is that which pleases God. Without faith one cannot please God.[7] There is no healing without faith being an active ingredient in the process of healing; whether

---

[7] Heb 11:6 But without faith it is impossible to please Him, for he who comes to God must believe that He is, and that He is a rewarder of those who diligently seek Him.

with the person being healed or the one administering healing. I will discuss this later.

Kingdom principles encompass everything in the kingdom of God and how they affect things in the natural realm.

Things like finances, soulish desires, and spiritual manifestations are all touched by kingdom principles. The laws of sowing and reaping, giving and receiving, and love and hate, etc. all function, either good or bad through kingdom principles.

If we, as Jesus did, function in kingdom principles, through faith, we will receive the same results He did. Healing is just one of those principles.

The picture of heaven

Most people accept the fact of heaven's goodness, perfection, and glory, but many struggle with the fact that heaven's reality should be a part of their experience.

Any astute student of God's word should have no problem believing that God wants the best for them. Their belief system should be able to assimilate Jesus' sermons to the point that they see past the superficial and to the meat of His lessons.

Those lessons were to teach that God wants what is in heaven to be a part of the listener's life. After-all that is the prayer He taught them!

Your kingdom come….

Jesus taught us that it was God's will that His kingdom come to the earth. The kingdom's government was to touch every aspect of human experience. Kingdom government should be the overriding factor in all wants, desires, and joys. *But seek first the kingdom of God and His righteousness, and all these things shall be added to you.* Matt 6:33

Jesus taught that what was in heaven should be in the earth. Those things in heaven were all good, all holy, and all life producing. In other words, He told us to bring what was in heaven to earth. We do this through faith and trust.

Jesus' life demonstrated the reality of His prayer. He, under the tutelage of the Holy Spirit, went about healing the sick, casting out demons, and bringing the good of heaven into the darkness of the sin infected world.

Your will be done On earth as it is in heaven….

Jesus taught that the only will that really mattered in life was the will of the Father. He went about doing only that which the Father desired through the leading of the Holy Spirit.

Jesus knew the will of the Father because He spent time with the Father in prayer and meditation. He taught His disciples to do the same.

It was through an understanding of the Father's will that He went about doing the Father's will as it was in heaven, but now in the earth.

Jesus knew He was the instrument of the Father to bring what was in heaven and God's will to the earth. He then taught mankind to do the same.

What is the Father's will?

I'm sure you have heard the well-meaning prayers of those who are seeking God use the term *"If it be thy will."* I don't mean to be hard or insensitive to someone's honest prayer, but I think we need to examine what we really believe before we pray those prayers.

Why is it that we have such a difficult time understanding God's will when it comes to healing? It isn't like we don't have anything to inform us; after-all, we have His written word. We have the accounts of Jesus' life and miracles which mirror the Father's will. Then there is the life changing experience of those who become children of God through the born-again experience. These are all part and parcel of God's will in action.

Jesus said, *"For I have come down from heaven, not to do My own will, but the will of Him who sent Me."* John 6:38

Since Jesus was doing the will of the Father it is obvious that God's will is to heal people.

Some accounts of the Father's will to heal through Jesus:

Matt 4:24 Then His fame went throughout all Syria; and they brought to Him all sick people who were afflicted with various diseases and torments, and those who were demon-possessed, epileptics, and paralytics; and He healed them.

Matt 12:15-1615 But when Jesus knew it, He withdrew from there. And great multitudes followed Him, and He healed them all.

Matt 15:30-31 Then great multitudes came to Him, having with them the lame, blind, mute, maimed, and many others; and they laid them down at Jesus' feet, and He healed them.

Matt 19:22 And great multitudes followed Him, and He healed them there.

Matt 21:14-15 Then the blind and the lame came to Him in the temple, and He healed them.

Luke 6:19 and the whole multitude sought to touch Him, for power went out from Him and healed them all.

It serves no good for anyone to assume God is so sovereign in His will that He can do anything He wants. Yes, God is sovereign, and He can do anything He wants, but He has limited Himself to His word. He goes to great length to ensure us that He responds to us according to His word. As a covenant keeping being He would never go against His pronounced word to His creation. His word is so important to Him that He has put above His very name.[8]

Therefore, God would never arbitrarily heal one and not the other. Jesus demonstrated this when He healed all who came to Him.

Jesus went about doing the will of the Father as a covenant keeping Son of God. He gave constant example that covenant with God and His covenant with man was very important and healing was part of that covenant to an obedient peoples.[9]

---

[8] Ps 138:2 I will worship toward Your holy temple, And praise Your name For Your lovingkindness and Your truth; For You have magnified Your word above all Your name. NKJV

[9] Deut 28:9 "The Lord will establish you as a holy people to Himself, just as He has sworn to you, if you keep the commandments of the Lord your God and walk in His ways. 10 Then all peoples of the earth shall see that you are called by the name of the Lord, and they shall be afraid of you. 11 And the Lord will grant you plenty of goods, in the fruit of your body, in the increase of your livestock, and in the produce of your ground, in the land of which the Lord swore to your fathers to give you. 12 The Lord will open to you His good treasure, the heavens, to give the rain to your land in its season, and to bless all the work of your hand. You shall lend to many nations, but you shall not borrow. 13 And the Lord will make you the head and not the tail; you shall be above only, and not be beneath, if you heed the commandments of the Lord your God, which I command you today, and are careful to observe them. 14 So you shall not turn aside from any of the words which I command you this day, to the right or the left, to go after other gods to serve them. NKJV

Suffice it to say, *it is the Father's will to heal ALL!* If it is not, then Jesus went about healing people against the Father's will.

5

The Ingredients of God's Will

Since we have established that it is God's will to heal people we must go beyond the *them* to the *me* in the equation of healing.

Usually people do not have a problem with others being healed, but we usually struggle with *me* being healed. We must come to the faith point in our belief system that we believe healing is for everyone.

Now, remember, we have seen that Jesus healed everyone who came to Him. It was the Father's will for them to be healed or Jesus would not have done it. That is established. Let's move on!

The first major ingredient in God's will for healing is faith; Jesus' faith, your faith, and other's faith.

Jesus' faith:

Jesus has faith to heal you because He believes the Father and does what the Father wants.

When Jesus ministered healing to people He presented Himself as God's word in flesh to the sick person and declared what was written about the situation. Since Jesus was the manifested word of God He declared with action that which the word declared, *He sent His word and healed them, And delivered them from their destructions.* Ps 107:20

Christ-like faith[10]: (Taken from, Dr. Roger Sapp's, *Christ Centered Healing Ministry Seminar, used by permission.*)

Christ-like faith, in Christ is the product of the real Gospel. What do these passages describe as "faith"?

***<u>Woman with the issue of blood.</u>** Matthew 9:22 But Jesus turning and seeing her said, "Daughter, take courage; your faith has made you well." And at once the woman was made well.*

---

[10] Dr. Roger Sapps *Christ Centered Healing Ministry Seminar,* Copyright 2006, Page 9, Chapter 4, *The Multitude Model Response.* All Nations Ministries & Publications, PO Box 620, Springtown, Texas 76082 USA, Secure Website: www.allnationsmin.org

What did the woman do that Jesus describes as "faith"? She came to Jesus with simple expectation.

Two blind men. *Matthew 9:29 Then He touched their eyes, saying, "Be it done to you according to your faith."*

What did these men do that Jesus is describing as "faith"? They were persistent and overcame difficulties. They came to Him for healing.

Canaanite woman's daughter. *Matthew 15:28 Then Jesus answered and said to her, "O woman, your faith is great; be it done for you as you wish." And her daughter was healed at once.* (See also Luke 5:20)

What action on the part of this woman does Jesus describe as "faith"? She came to Christ for help for her daughter and would not give up.

Four men's faith. *Mark 2:5 And Jesus seeing their faith said to the paralytic, "My son, your sins are forgiven."* (The man was healed.)

What action on the part of these men is Jesus describing as "faith"? They revealed their faith by overcoming the difficulties of bringing their friend to Jesus.

Blind Bartimaeus healed. *Mark 10:52 And Jesus said to him, "Go your way; your faith has made you well." And immediately he regained his sight and began following Him on the road.*

What action on the part of Bartimaeus is Jesus describing as "faith". He overcame the discouragement of the crowd and came to Jesus for help.

The Samaritan, one of the ten lepers healed. *Luke 17:19 And He said to him, "Rise, and go your way; your faith has made you well."*

What action did all of the lepers do that caused them to be healed and caused Jesus to describe it as "faith"? They came to Jesus.

Unnamed blind man in Jericho. *Luke 18:42 And Jesus said to him, "Receive your sight; your faith has made you well."*

What action of the part of the man did Jesus describe as "faith"? The man cried out persistently to Jesus and would not be discouraged by the multitude until he was able to come to Jesus for healing.

Failures in healing described as lack of faith.
Jesus *in His Hometown Nazareth. Matthew 13:58*

And He did not do many miracles there because of their unbelief

Unbelief is from the Greek word that means literally "no faith". What didn't these people do that Matthew is describing as "unbelief'? They didn't come to Jesus for help because they didn't believe in Him.

Your faith:

We must never forget that we have a part to play in the reality of healing. Our faith, both as a person who may need healing, or when we are administering healing, must be an active ingredient in the process.

Remember, without faith it is impossible to please God.[11] Your faith must be founded upon something you know to be true. Faith is the substance of things hoped for and the evidence of things not seen.[12] Substance comes as we walk with God for some time and have found Him faithful and trusting. Evidence is seen realities that

---

[11] Heb 11:6 But without faith it is impossible to please Him, for he who comes to God must believe that He is, and that He is a rewarder of those who diligently seek Him.

[12] Heb 11:1 Now faith is the substance of things hoped for, the evidence of things not seen.

have touched our lives when we trusted God. It was tangible and rewarding even in the light of the unseen at the time.

Faith takes God at His word which states that by Jesus' strips we were healed. [13] We must be convinced it is the Father's will to heal us.

Jesus must be the focus of our faith. It can't be faith in healing for healing sake; it must be in what Jesus did for us on the cross.

Other's faith:

When we administer healing to someone they may or may not have an active believing faith in God and His will or desire to heal them.

Scripture tells us that God is not a respecter of persons and what He will do for one He will do for all. This truth must become a part of every person's life.

Jesus healed people based upon their faith, their friend's faith, and His faith. In each case He ministered love and understanding to them in order

---

[13] 1 Peter 2:24 who Himself bore our sins in His own body on the tree, that we, having died to sins, might live for righteousness — by whose stripes you were healed.

for them to see beyond the immediate to the end result of healing. One time He asked, *Do you believe;* another time He said, *Only believe,* and another time He said nothing but made mud of spit and administered the healing. Faith became a reality to the person after the fact in most cases.

A good example of someone else's faith being the catalyst to heal was when four friends came to Jesus carrying their friend on his bed.

"And again He entered Capernaum after some days, and it was heard that He was in the house. Immediately many gathered together, so that there was no longer room to receive them, not even near the door. And He preached the word to them. Then they came to Him, bringing a paralytic who was carried by four men. And when they could not come near Him because of the crowd, they uncovered the roof where He was. So when they had broken through, they let down the bed on which the paralytic was lying. When Jesus saw their faith, He said to the paralytic, "Son, your sins are forgiven you." And some of the scribes were sitting there and reasoning in their hearts, "Why does this Man speak blasphemies like this? Who can forgive sins but God alone?" But immediately,

when Jesus perceived in His spirit that they reasoned thus within themselves, He said to them, "Why do you reason about these things in your hearts? Which is easier, to say to the paralytic, 'Your sins are forgiven you,' or to say, 'Arise, take up your bed and walk'? But that you may know that the Son of Man has power on earth to forgive sins" — *He said to the paralytic, "I say to you, arise, take up your bed, and go to your house." Immediately he arose, took up the bed, and went out in the presence of them all, so that all were amazed and glorified God, saying, "We never saw anything like this!" Mark 2:1-12 NKJV*

- ✓ Apparently the sick man did not have faith for healing; but his friends did!
- ✓ Jesus recognized the four friend's faith
- ✓ The only people present who had a problem with the healing and the reward of faith were the religious leaders.
- ✓ Apparently the man's sickness was caused by sin, which Jesus forgave, and then the man was healed.

Faith of the four friends not only was the catalyst for the man's healing it was the catalyst for the man's sins to be forgiven.

The second major ingredient in God's will for healing is trust.

Trust takes God at His word and does not permit the physical look of present problems to dictate one's faith because one has walked with God for some time.

The secret lies in *putting this truth into practice,* by making it such a powerful theme in your life that you view every event, every sorrow, every prayer with the unshakable conviction that God is totally, spotlessly trustworthy.

That's where we mess up. We want to trust in *anything* rather than the Lord. We'll trust in our own abilities, in our boss's judgment of us, in our money, our doctor, even in an airline pilot. But the Lord? Well... it's easy to trust in things we can see. Sure, we *believe* in God, but to allow him to run our life? That's asking a little too much, we think.

Trusting God for a healing when we can't see God stretches our faith, our belief system, and goes contrary to the world's way of thinking. After all, the world tells us we must trust in medicine, doctors, and pills. But God tells us to just childlike trust Him.

Deal with the doubt.[14] (Taken from, Dr. Roger Sapp's, *Christ Centered Healing Ministry Seminar, used by permission.*)

What is Doubt? Most Christians have not identified their doubts because they don't understand doubt. The Greek word for doubt is also frequently translated as *judge*. Doubt is *judging yourself or someone else outside the grace of God*.

Doubt is making yourself or someone else a *special exception*. Doubt is *discrimination* against yourself or others. Doubt is *disqualifying* yourself or making yourself the *special exception*. Doubt is an idea that is an a*lternative* to faith. If true faith comes to Jesus in simplicity to receive from Him, then doubt is the primary reason why many Christians do not come to Him. For example someone might say: *I can pray for others and they*

---

[14] Dr. Roger Sapps *Christ Centered Healing Ministry Seminar,* Copyright 2006, Page 13. All Nations Ministries & Publications, PO Box 620, Springtown, Texas 76082 USA, Secure Website: www.allnationsmin.org

will be healed but I can't get healed myself. This is disqualifying yourself making you the special exception.

The New Testament reveals the problem of doubt.

Peter walking on the water. *Matthew 14:31 "O you of little faith, why did you doubt?" What did the disciples learn from this situation? They learned that the power of God to do this miracle was dependent upon Peter's resistance to doubting. We find the same thing is true about healing.*

Cursing the Fig Tree. *Matthew 21:21 "Truly I say to you, if you have faith and do not doubt, you shall not only do what was done to the fig tree, but even if you say to this mountain, Be taken up and cast into the sea', it shall happen. "* Jesus tells the disciples that they can do small miracles like the fig tree and larger miracles but they must deal with doubt. Retranslating/reconsidering the meaning of the key phrase in this passage: *If you have faith and do not disqualify yourself (or someone else, you can do miracles like this. If you have faith and don't judge yourself outside the grace of God, you can have a consistent ministry of healing. If you* *have faith and don't discriminate against yourself for a reason, you can experience what twelve ordinary men who followed Jesus Christ experienced. If you have faith and don't think that you are the mysterious special exception, you can receive what others receive.*

About wisdom*. James 1:5-8 But if any of you lacks wisdom, let him ask of God, who gives to all men generously and without reproach, and it will be given to him. But let him ask in faith without any doubting, for the one who doubts is like the surf of the sea driven and tossed by the wind. For let not that man expect that he will receive anything of the Lord, being a double-minded man, unstable in all his ways.*

James tells us that doubting will prevent us from receiving from the Lord. It will create two minds in us that will make us unstable. We get rid of one of these minds by obtaining the mind of Christ.

Appraisal through the mind of Christ. *1 Corinthians 2:15-16 But he who is spiritual appraises all things, yet he himself is appraised by no man. For WHO HAS KNOWN THE MIND OF*

THE LORD, THAT HE SHOULD INSTRUCT HIM? But we have the mind of Christ.

What is the mind of Christ? It is not some mystical thing that we acquire in a more mystical way. The disciples had the mind of Christ because they walked and talked with Him on a daily basis. The mind of Christ is simply thinking about things in the way that Jesus Christ thought about them. We obtain the mind of Christ by meditation on Christ in the Gospels. We need to see what the Twelve disciples saw. If we can understand what the Twelve disciples understood about Jesus and healing, then we will have their experience of healing. We then appraise spiritual ideas presented to us by what Jesus taught and demonstrated of the Father's will.

First Common Doubt: It may not be God's will to heal. This idea is appraised and measured by knowing Jesus Christ. Jesus demonstrated the perfect will of the Father. He healed everyone in a multitude several times. (Matthew 8:16, 12:15, Luke 6:19, Acts 5:16, Acts 10:38) The disciples knew by observing Christ that God's will was certain, reliable, predictable and unchanging in the arena of healing. The will of God is certain. Father wants to heal all.

The New Testament teaches that God is not a respecter of persons. God shows no partiality, no favoritism and no preference of one person over another. The disciples saw this as Christ ministered to the multitudes. Christ drew no distinctions between those who came to Him.

Second Common Doubt: God has a purpose for this sickness. This doubt is produced when believers assign a divine purpose to sickness. It is so common to be a cultural norm in the Church.

List of common purposes:

God may be using or allowing this sickness in my life to...Teach me something. Ask what have you learned? Most cannot come up with anything despite the fact that they may have been sick for years.

Improve my character. Actually most people don't become more Christ-like by being sick. Sometimes they become discouraged, sometimes they lose their faith, become angry, and bitter. Long-term sickness tends to reveal what is actually there in character but does not improve it.

People of strong Christian character are revealed by long-term sickness as patient and good. People of poor character are revealed as impatient, angry and vindictive. Jesus never indicated by teaching or action that God wouldn't heal someone because of a dealing going on in their character. The Twelve disciples would not have accepted this idea.

Test me. There was no test revealed in the New Testament except coming to Jesus. True faith has nothing to prove to anyone. It simply comes to Christ. Jesus never indicated to anyone that they needed to pass a test in order to be healed. The Twelve disciples would have rejected the idea that you must pass a test in order to be healed.

Discipline me. You don't discipline your children with sickness, injury or chronic pain. Why should we project this idea on God? Jesus never indicated that someone could not receive healing because they were being disciplined by God. The apostle Peter would have rejected this idea because He never saw Jesus refuse to heal the most wicked sinner that had come to Him for healing.

Judge me for sin. Jesus healed the good and the bad without discrimination. He often forgave them their sins in the process of healing them. While sin may create sickness in us, coming to Christ in simple faith and repentance insures forgiveness of sins and healing. The disciples knew that Christ was not withholding healing because of sin.

Slow me down. Jesus did not withhold healing from people because they needed to rest or were living too fast a lifestyle. Christ did not withhold healing from someone because they needed time with God. It is rather obvious that sickness is not a good way to rest. God has more productive, less destructive, ways to get our attention.

A divine and benevolent mystery. Jesus Christ does not reveal that God wishes someone to remain sick due to a mystery. His disciples would not have known this idea. They would have known that those who come in simplicity to Jesus for help get that help and those who don't come for some reason, don't get that help.

Be glorified in sickness. Jesus Christ does not reveal that sickness glorifies God. He never left anyone sick who came to Him because it was glorifying God. He healed everyone who came to Him. This reveals that healing of sickness glorifies

God not sickness itself. These purposes must be measured by Jesus Christ's response to people. Christ does not reveal a purpose for sickness. He never suggested any of these ideas. He never hesitated to heal. He never turned anyone away because God's purpose was for them to stay ill.

This is what the disciple learned of God's will from hearing and observing Jesus Christ as He revealed the Father.

Bad Interpretations of Job's sufferings and Paul's thorn in the flesh create doubt. We should learn about New Covenant healing from Christ not Job. However, we will consider Job because misunderstanding Job has created doubt for people. The devil made Job sick. God healed Him. Most people don't know that Job was healed and lived to be 140 years old. You are not having a Job's experience if you remain sick. There are 38 chapters of Job's friends blaming him and Job blaming God. No one ever blames the devil.

Traditional Idea: Job was sick for a long time may be wrong. 38 chapters consist of one unending conversation between Job and his friends followed by a conversation between God and Job. Job's friends arrived after they heard that he was sick and remained with him for a week. The whole experience described in the book of Job could have taken place in a few weeks.

Many attribute the devil's work to God by bad reasoning. Thoughts go like this: *God allowed devil to make Job sick, this must be what God wants. What God allows must be His will.* Consider this idea in other matters. God is allowing: people to sin, people to die without Christ, marriages to break up. God is allowing children to die of disease and malnutrition.

Does God want these things? No! We must measure the will of God by Jesus Christ who is the light of the world and not by the spiritual darkness of fallen angels, demons and unregenerate humanity. God wishes to save, heal and deliver. He wants abundant life for humanity.

He wants righteousness, peace and joy in the Holy Spirit for people.

Paul's thorn in the flesh. 2 Corinthians 12:7-10. Paul says that he was given *surpassing revelations. As* a result of these revelations, he was given a thorn in the flesh a *messenger* of Satan *(aggellos-* transliterated *angel.)* Most people would not qualify for a thorn no matter what it may be simply because they are not having abundant revelations.

The context of the passage is about hardships, not sickness. The Greek word translated *thorn is* found only in this passage in the New Testament. However, this Greek word *skolop is* used twice about enemies in the Septuagint (the Greek Old Testament). This Greek word is not used about sickness at all anywhere. Therefore, a better interpretation of Paul's thorn is *a fallen angel that stirred up persecution against Paul wherever he went.* Paul might have been sick at times but he could receive healing like the rest of us. (There is a more detailed explanation in Dr. Sapp's books on healing.)

Third Common Doubt: Maybe this is not God's time to heal.

When is the right time to be healed? What did Jesus demonstrate to His disciples? He healed the people in the multitudes when they came. The multitudes decided the timing. The timing was in their hands, not his. Now is the right time to be healed.

What about measuring the timing idea by Jesus Christ's message? Jesus said *The Kingdom is at hand.* Christ's message meant that the Kingdom was happening then. He demonstrated that this was true by healing then. Now is the right time to be healed.

Fourth Common Doubt: Maybe I lack faith to be healed. Our experience tells us that faith is not generally the problem among Christians but doubt is a very real problem. Once doubt is identified and captured, then many simply are able to come to Christ with confidence and receive their healing.

Faith is not a thing that you produce by trying to make something happen. The faith that receives healing is faith in the person of Jesus Christ. It is not faith that God heals that heals the sick. That is simply intellectual assent to the facts of the New Testament. The object of biblical faith is Jesus Christ. Therefore, faith/believing comes by hearing a faithful presentation of the gospel that reveals Jesus Christ as Healer.

Faith is a fruit of the Spirit and a gift of the Spirit. Everyone is given a measure of faith that must ultimately rest on Jesus Christ. All that is needed is a mustard seed of faith in Christ to move a mountain.

A Christ-Centered Confession of Faith: *This healing belongs to me because of what Jesus has done.*

6

Man Doesn't Live By Bread Alone

Matt 4:4 But He answered and said, "It is written, 'Man shall not live by bread alone, but by every word that proceeds from the mouth of God.'" NKJV

Isa 55:11 So shall My word be that goes forth from My mouth; It shall not return to Me void, But it shall accomplish what I please, And it shall prosper in the thing for which I sent it. NKJV

I have quoted many scriptures giving proof of God's desire to heal, both in the old and new testaments. Those scriptures give accounts of healing which not only tell the story of those who were healed, but they are given to us from God to convince us.

However, if one does not believe the authenticity of scripture one would disregard the healing accounts all together. It is imperative that we totally believe the Bible as God's factual thoughts toward us and how He desires for us to live with Him.

It isn't enough to read, know, and accept the stories, either historically or spiritually. One must move past those things to seeing the truth which each story gives. It must become life sustaining bread to us!

Many years ago I was teaching in a small home Bible study when the Holy Spirit told me to *stop reading the Bible like a dime store novel.* Apparently I had accepted the Bible and its stories as true and historically factual, but I had not taken the truths that each taught to the point that it sustained, nourished, and matured me.

God wanted me to become more mature. He wanted me to take in the truths of His word and find that it gave life to me. He wanted me to know that what God said in all of His promises would come to those who truly believe.

It has to be personal!

All too often we say we believe scripture, and believe the accounts as they happened to others, but we fail to believe them for self.

We must come to the point with scripture that we truly believe that the message in it is for us! The story of the Bible is God (we get the word history from *His Story*), it tells us about God, what He did, does, and will do; and it tells us how we can relate to, and receive from Him.

Healing will elude us if we do not believe or make scripture personal to us. When scripture tells us that God is no respecter of persons we must believe that what He did for someone else He will do for me.

We must accept that what the Bible shows us about a healing event is teaching us to associate with the truth of the event and then receive its results as it was ours.; keeping in mind that God is the same yesterday, today, and forever. What He does for one He will do for all who believe.

When God tells someone in the scripture to repent, we must repent. When He tells someone to obey, we must obey. When He tells someone to turn from sin or the course they are on, we must make sure we are doing the right thing as well. If we fail, we suffer the consequence of disobedience, and our health can suffer because we open the door to the enemy and ravages of a sin infected world.

So, we must make scripture truths personal. We must believe the accounts of scripture healings as a teaching tool for our healing.

To make scripture nourishing bread to us we must not only take it in by reading, we must believe it (eat), internalize it (digest), and let it nourish (do something with it) us.

Believe:

Now, it is most important that we truly believe the Bible. Either we believe that the Bible is the very word of God or we don't. We must believe that the truths of the Bible are God given and every event recorded for our edification has eternal and earthly consequences.

We must believe that when God, His Son, or the Holy Spirit tells us something, it is every bit true, reliable, and effective for our lives.

We must believe that the promises of God are very definitely yes and amen.[15] We then claim them as our own and faithfully receive them.

---

[15] 2 Cor 1:20 For all the promises of God in Him are Yes, and in Him Amen, to the glory of God through us .NKJV

Internalize:

Internalizing or digesting the word of God is more than just reading scripture; it is mediating on its truths to the point that they become satisfying to our soul and spirit.

When we take in natural food we become satisfied and it affects our physical bodies to the point that we feel healthy, strong, and refreshed. It is the same with spiritual food of scripture; it affects our spirit and soul to the point that we become stronger and more active to the point that we ward off anything that would try to destroy.

Nourish:

The test of nourishment is its reality to make us healthy and strong. However, the true test of spiritual nourishment is what we do with the truths we have taken in. If we are not using the truths of the scripture we have not really been nourished. We must act upon it!

It is in the doing that scripture becomes food to us. As we take in God's word about healing (or any other subject), as we believe its truths, and then act upon it through faith, we become recipients of that truth in our bodies.

It shall accomplish what I please:

God promises that His word will accomplish what He pleases. We have discussed that it is God's will that healing take place in the earth. We have seen that it was God's will that Jesus made it possible for us to be healed; it is a part of the atoning sacrifice of Jesus, just as much as salvation. We have seen that God is no respecter of persons, so it is His will to heal anyone. Therefore, we must accept the fact that because God made healing possible through Jesus, we can and are a recipient of healing when needed.

We must once and for all establish in our heart, mind, and soul that it is the word of God, established through Jesus, finalized with the cross and resurrection, that healing is mine because God said so!

Jesus, being the living word of God, has come to establish the Father's will and word of healing to all who will accept. Therefore, it will prosper in my life because God said it should prosper in me as I believe. It will also accomplish in me what the Father intended it to do for me.

7

The Children's Bread

Matt 15:21-28 Then Jesus went out from there and departed to the region of Tyre and Sidon. 22 And behold, a woman of Canaan came from that region and cried out to Him, saying, "Have mercy on me, O Lord, Son of David! My daughter is severely demon-possessed." 23 But He answered her not a word. And His disciples came and urged Him, saying, "Send her away, for she cries out after us." 24 But He answered and said, "I was not sent except to the lost sheep of the house of Israel." 25 Then she came and worshiped Him, saying, "Lord, help me!" 26 But He answered and said, "It is not good to take the children's bread and throw it to the little dogs." 27 And she said, "Yes, Lord, yet even the little dogs eat the crumbs which fall from their masters' table." 28 Then Jesus answered and said to her, "O woman, great is

your faith! Let it be to you as you desire." And her daughter was healed from that very hour. NKJV

Jesus gave us some very important information about healing in the above verses. First, He told us that healing was the children's bread. Second, He told us that healing would come to those who have faith. And third, He told us our faith would bring about what we desired about healing. Fourth, He told us that He was first to minister to the lost sheep of the house of Israel.

Who are the children?

Jesus told us that He was sent to the house of Israel first. He was fulfilling the requirements of the law which stated that salvation was first meant for the Hebrew people and then to the Gentiles (those who are not Jews).

Obviously, the children were the Hebrew people, but they would not receive unless they too believed through faith; however, whether the Jew received or not did not diminish the fact that healing was part of God's plan for His children.

Under the New Covenant Jesus has made anyone who believes through faith a child of

God,[16] and as a child of God is entitled to the bread that the Father gives His children; in this case that bread is healing.

It stands to reason then, that God has made provision for healing for all of His children. If you are born-again, you are a child of God and healing is one of the rights you can walk in.

Is the bread only healing?

No, is the simple answer! But, as with anything in the kingdom of God, we must possess it through faith and action.

Since we are using the analogy of bread let's look at it this way. When bread is presented at your table you have a choice to eat or not; no one at the table will force you.

God doesn't force you to eat healing either, you can receive freely as His child or you can refuse, but it does not diminish the fact that as a child of God, healing as with many things in the kingdom of God, is still available to you.

---

[16] John 1:11 He came to His own, and His own did not receive Him. 12 But as many as received Him, to them He gave the right to become children of God, to those who believe in His name: 13 who were born, not of blood, nor of the will of the flesh, nor of the will of man, but of God. NKJV

Can non-children eat the bread?

It is interesting in the above account that when Jesus' disciples wanted to send the woman away Jesus didn't respond to that request. It was like He wanted the encounter to take place and more to transpire than her just being an annoyance. It was obvious that it was a time for teaching, miracles, and compassion.

Often, we disciples see situations as an annoyance instead of an opportunity for healing and miracles. We need to be more sensitive to the leading of the Holy Spirit for one of God's children to be healed.

Remember, the Canaanite woman was not a Jew; she was not one of the "Children" and therefore outside of the family and all of its provision. However, Jesus' whole purpose in being born was to bring mankind back to the fold of Father God. The Canaanite woman was obviously a candidate for this.

There are those we meet who are not children of God because they have not been born-again and are outside of the promises of God, but they are candidates for that privilege. Once they are ministered to and receive healing they too may turn to the Lord for salvation.

Remember, faith is what pleases and moves God. He always responds to faith! So, anyone who comes to Him, in faith, and humility receives.

When Jesus told the woman **"It is not good to take the children's bread and throw it to the little dogs."** he was stating a fact that healing was for the children, but He was not excluding her or anyone who would call on that bread through faith. **"O woman, great is your faith! Let it be to you as you desire."**

Jesus took the bread of the children, gave it to a person in need, because that is what loving, accepting, and forgiving children of God do. The Canaanite woman may not have been a child of the promise in that regard, but she was a candidate for the kingdom of God and the family of God.

Jesus didn't differentiate between a Jew and a Gentile when it came to healing and forgiveness. Anyone who came to Him He healed! Yes, the bread of healing was first for the Children of God, but anyone could call on the feeding as their need dictated.

Who qualifies for healing?

Doubt is *disqualifying* yourself, or making yourself the *special exception*.

When Jesus walked the earth and went about teaching the kingdom of God and the gospel (The Good News) He gave proof positive of the Father's will pertaining to healing. Healed ALL who came to Him for healing! No one was left out.

Picture the settings in which Jesus performed healing to the multitudes. In all cases when either tens, thousands, or one individual was present He healed without discrimination as to the spiritual makeup of the person. It didn't matter if there was saint or sinner, self-righteous or humble, beggar or business man, priest or pauper; all were healed.

Jesus didn't tell people to repent before He would heal them. He didn't tell them to go and get their life straight before they were worthy of healing. He didn't turn anyone away because they may have committed some form of inappropriate behavior. He didn't tell them to get saved before healing, He just told them that the kingdom of God had arrived and healing was a part of that kingdom.

All men/women are lost and without hope, Jesus came to change all that. His presence gave proof of a loving God, a caring Father, and healing Lord. No one was left out, ignored, or overlooked for healing. The very reality of healing was a convincing proof that God loved them and that He was real; their healing would bring not only joy and liberty, it would bring conviction of sin enough so to bring them to repentance and salvation.

So, to answer the question "Who is qualified for healing?" Everyone, all peoples, no one left out; saint and sinner, rogue and rascal, the drunk and dignified, witch and wealthy, and the humble as well as the repentant. EVERYONE is qualified for healing!

After receiving healing people would repent, turn from their wicked ways and seek out God. The healing was proof positive that there was a God, He cared, and He wanted holiness, righteousness, as well as joy and freedom. God's goodness, forbearance, and longsuffering demonstrated through Jesus, by means of healing, without the demand of repentance brought the very repentance that God requires for salvation.[17]

No distinction

Jesus made no distinction between anyone when He healed all who came to Him. In the crowds standing before Jesus He never signaled anyone out and denied them healing because of sin, unworthiness, or shortcoming, He just healed all who came to Him.

In other words;

- If you needed healing you were qualified for healing.
- If you were weak and heavy laden you were qualified for healing.
- If you needed rest from discomfort, confusion, and pain you were qualified.
- If you needed healing with hearing, seeing, touching, walking, internal body function, or any others disease and sickness you were qualified.

---

[17] Or do you despise the riches of His goodness, forbearance, and longsuffering, not knowing that the goodness of God leads you to repentance? Rom 2:4-5 NKJV

- If you hated your neighbor, cursed, drank, smoked, were an adulterer, believed in other gods, or were not a Jew you were qualified.

Why are we all qualified?

Because Jesus loves all people! Because God sent His Son to give demonstration that God hates sickness and the devastation it causes in the earth. Because God wants all people to know and realize that Jesus is the only way to salvation and eternity with God. Healing was and is a means to demonstrate God's love for us.

When we go to Jesus for healing; in faith, without doubt and child-like belief, we can receive just because we are the object of God's love and affection. Our healing gives proof positive that God loves us and then leads to repentance, forgiveness, and acceptance.

8

The Commission

Mark 16:15 And He said to them, "Go into all the world and preach the gospel to every creature. 16 He who believes and is baptized will be saved; but he who does not believe will be condemned. 17 And these signs will follow those who believe: In My name they will cast out demons; they will speak with new tongues; 18 they will take up serpents; and if they drink anything deadly, it will by no means hurt them; they will lay hands on the sick, and they will recover." NKJV

Healing is a part of the great commission to see people not only saved, but made whole in all aspects of their lives.

Jesus told us that the gospel must be preached; the gospel entails more than just salvation. Baptism is an ingredient of salvation, belief is a must, demons are to be dealt with, power to speak in tongues, and dealing with anything that would try to kill the one bringing the message of the gospel is all part and parcel in the gospel.

This writing is not intended to teach on demons, tongues, deadly poisons, or snakes (and, no, I don't believe we should tempt God with snake handling), but it is intended to teach on the commission of going with the gospel and healing the sick.

Why is healing so important to the gospel? Because it was important to Jesus!

Jesus went about healing all who came to Him. He taught about the kingdom of God with signs and wonders. He made a point to demonstrate that the kingdom of God was good, and included health and healing. Therefore, it stands to reason that the commission given to the disciples, and we are included, was the same as His commission from the Father. That commission was the gospel of forgiveness, acceptance through faith, and healing.

Every child commissioned!

It is so very important that we understand our calling as children of God. Every one of us who is born-again, who confesses Jesus as Lord, and who believes our home is heaven has been commissioned to do the same things Jesus did.

There may be individuals in the body of Christ who have the special gifting of healing[18] that they operate on a regular basis, but every child of God has been called to operate in healing as they go with the gospel to others.

We must see healing as part of the gospel that gives evidence of God's will for each person. Healing gives proof that God cares and understands the ravages of this world. When we administer healing to others, they are open to the gospel and the message of forgiveness.

Healing, as a sign

When Jesus healed all those who came to Him He freely gave in order that the healing would be a sign of God's love and compassion. When we go about healing people it is a sign that Jesus is who He claims, God cares, and there is a provision from God to do so.

---

[18] 1 Cor 12:28 And in the church God has appointed first of all apostles, second prophets, third teachers, then workers of miracles, also those having gifts of healing, NIV

Supernatural signs, in Jesus name, always give proof of the salvation message and make it possible for the weak in faith to believe.

With the commission come gifts

It is important to keep in mind that Jesus would not have sent the disciples out to preach the kingdom of God and to do the many signs and wonders if they were not equipped to do so.

Jesus' name:

Each born-again person carries the name of Jesus as authority from God. This authoritative mandate is as if each believer was deputized by God Himself. Each is God's representative going into life's situations with the power to change it for the glory of God and the betterment of mankind. **Luke 10:19 Behold, I give you the authority to trample on serpents and scorpions, and over all the power of the enemy, and nothing shall by any means hurt you. NKJV**

Acts 3:6 Then Peter said, "Silver and gold I do not have, but what I do have I give you: In the name of Jesus Christ of Nazareth, rise up and walk." 7 And he took him by the right hand and

lifted him up, and immediately his feet and ankle bones received strength. NKJV

Freely given spiritual authority

Luke 10:17 Then the seventy returned with joy, saying, "Lord, even the demons are subject to us in Your name." 18 And He said to them, "I saw Satan fall like lightning from heaven. 19 Behold, I give you the authority.... NKJV

Matt 10:7 And as you go, preach, saying, 'The kingdom of heaven is at hand.' 8 Heal the sick, cleanse the lepers, raise the dead, cast out demons. Freely you have received, freely give. NKJV

Each believer must have an established belief in the authority they have from God. As His child they are to represent Him in all realms with the power necessary to accomplish the task of evangelizing a lost and hurting world.

The authority the believer has is sufficient to each task, challenge, and obstacle. It is the same authority Jesus had and will bring the same results that Jesus realized. **Matt 21:21 So Jesus answered and said to them, "Assuredly, I say to you, if you have faith and do not doubt, you will**

not only do what was done to the fig tree, but also if you say to this mountain, 'Be removed and be cast into the sea,' it will be done. 22 And whatever things you ask in prayer, believing, you will receive." NKJV

As we go about representing the Father, as Jesus went about representing Him, we must be assured we have His approval and authority. Establishing in our hearts that we have been commissioned by God with authority to see people healed will strengthen our resolve to do so.

9

Conclusion

The conclusion of this book will end very simple with just a few directions:

One – Believe; believe the Lord who saved you is the same Lord who heals you.

Two – Accept; accept the fact that you are qualified to be healed. If you would have been present over two thousand years ago, with the multitudes that Jesus healed, you too would have been healed. Since Jesus is the same, yesterday, today and forever you are qualified to be healed now.

Three – Act; act upon the atoning reality of Jesus' sacrifice for you and appropriate it through faith. Faith in Jesus and faith that receives the healing before you see it.

Four – Release; release yourself from any doubt that either blames you, something else, or someone else for the sickness.

Five – Appropriate; appropriate the healing for yourself or others by a simple trust in God and what He gave you through His Son.

Six – Declare; declare your healing... *This healing belongs to me because of what Jesus has done.*

www.ingramcontent.com/pod-product-compliance
Lightning Source LLC
Chambersburg PA
CBHW071326040426
42444CB00009B/2099